"Perhaps the best writing on h... crossed my desk. A feast of acceptance and grace!"

—**Suzanne Stabile,** author of *The Path Between Us* and host of the podcast "The Enneagram Journey"

"*Love Love Bakery* is a space where the people in the neighborhood experience acceptance and love with a side of coffee and freshly baked bread."

—**Grace P. Cho,** Writer and Editorial Manager at (in)courage

"Communities of belonging happen wherever people make room for each other... like at Love Love Bakery, where kindness floats on the air like wild yeast."

—**Rev. Dr. Katie Hays,** Galileo Church

"A perfect glimpse into the slightly chaotic daily life of a local bakery."

—**Maggie Bailey,** Bramble & Bee

"The book is open to all, especially to little ones. It sings the praises of work done well."

—**Dr. David Naugle,** Dallas Baptist University, author of *Worldview: The History of a Concept*

H2
Alaska

To Teif,with love!

San Tricna
Mitchell

LOVE LOVE BAKERY

A WILD HOME FOR ALL

SARA TRIANA MITCHELL   ILLUSTRATIONS BY H2 ALASKA

To Jane, Mitch, and the music makers.
And to Anabelle, Clementine, and the mess makers.

In memory of Chuck Thompson, forever an early bird.
—Sara

To the Great Oak School community—teachers, administrators, parents, and the children I have had the pleasure to work with. Thank you for supporting and inspiring me every day.
—Hayley

Love Love Bakery: A Wild Home for All

Hand lettering by Sarah Keilers.

Cover design by Sarah Keilers, Sarah Hanna, H2 Alaska, Sara Triana Mitchell, and Lucid Books.

Copyright © 2018 by Sara Triana Mitchell

Published by Lucid Books in Houston, TX

www.LucidBooksPublishing.com

ISBN-13: 978-1-63296-197-6
ISBN-10: 1-63296-197-0
eISBN-13: 978-1-63296-198-3
eISBN-10: 1-63296-198-9

Special Sales: Most Lucid Books titles are available in special quantity discounts.
Custom imprinting or excerpting can also be done to fit special needs. Contact Lucid Books at Info@LucidBooksPublishing.com.

Jane and John are bakers and friends. They brew coffee and bake bread in an old blue house under a thick oak tree.

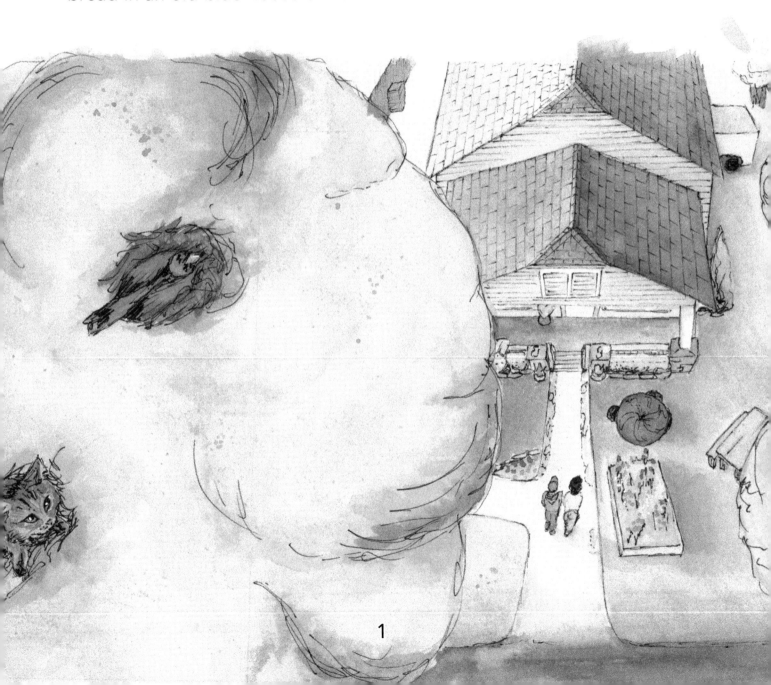

1

Today, the bakers and baristas will pour eight gallons of milk, grind 15 pounds of **coffee beans**, and crack 228 eggs.

They will measure 80 teaspoons of salt, 150 cups of flour, and 640 tablespoons of butter.

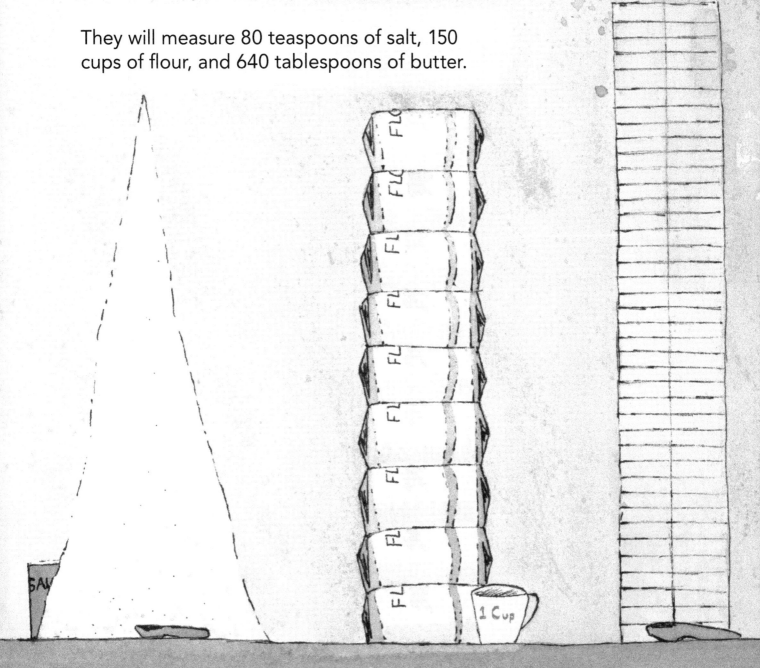

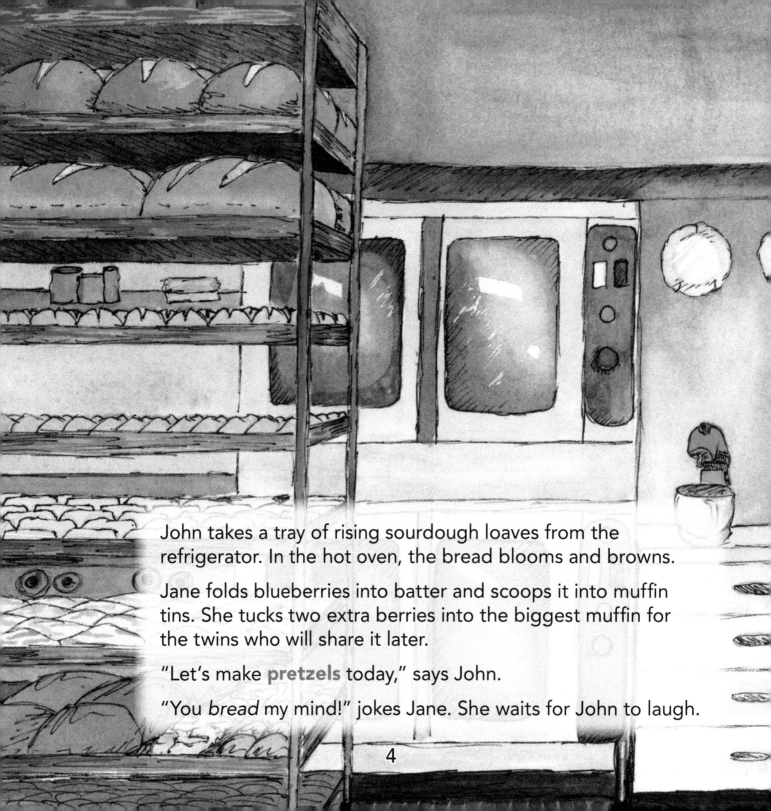

John takes a tray of rising sourdough loaves from the refrigerator. In the hot oven, the bread blooms and browns.

Jane folds blueberries into batter and scoops it into muffin tins. She tucks two extra berries into the biggest muffin for the twins who will share it later.

"Let's make **pretzels** today," says John.

"You *bread* my mind!" jokes Jane. She waits for John to laugh.

John just rolls out pie crust—cold and buttery. They bake pretzels and cinnamon rolls, too. The floured air floats out of the kitchen.

Jane's son Leo walks to the bakery when he wakes up. He grabs his favorite mug and sits on the front porch sipping a warm **morning drink** while he munches toast.

Leo's friends pop by before school.

"What are you eating?" Hafsa asks.

"Sourdough," says Leo.

"Sourdough?" asks her brother Hamza. "Sour like a pickle?"

"No, **sourdough bread** is just flour, salt, water, and starter. Starter is a gooey lump of flour that's kind of alive," says Leo.

"Alive?" asks Hamza.

"Yeah, starter sits in a jar on the counter and attracts wild yeast. Wild yeast is everywhere. In flour. In the air."

They look around, but the wild yeast in the air is too small to see.

"When you see the starter bubble and grow in the jar, it's working. So, then you mix all the ingredients up. Knead the dough. And the yeast makes the bread dough rise."

"Weird," says Hafsa.

"It's rad," says Leo.

7

Jane brings Leo's friends a blueberry muffin, sliced in half and ready to go. "Have a beautiful day," she says as the three of them leave for school.

8

"Hey, Mom?" calls Leo. "Try not to let things go nuts today."

Jane laughs. "Just a little bit nuts?"

Inside, the **barista** brews **coffee** and steams milk to make a latte.

10

When the sky has ripened to tangerine, Jane flips the front door sign. "All Are Welcome," it says in every color.

As she does, the first customer rides up.

"Good morning!" says Jane. "How was your bike ride?"

"Fantastic," he says. His mug of **espresso** and sweet **cream** waits for him.

12

Soon, the front door is swinging—open and close, open and close—on the rasping hinges. Everyone is ready for breakfast and coffee. The barista makes drinks one after another.

The flower shop owner from next door brings in a bucket of blossoms. After she orders her toast and tea, she arranges bouquets in jelly jars and places one on every table. The friendly petals wave hello.

13

Everyone who comes inside finds a place to settle.

"Welcome, welcome!" says Jane to the early birds carrying their newspapers and puzzles.

"Another all-nighter of painting? Here's your **kombucha**," she says to an artist dolloped with paint.

"Hello there, Molly! No shoes today?"
The bakery cat examines Molly's bare feet.

"What's up, pups!" says Jane to the
neighborhood dog gang.

15

What a thrill to be known! It feels like someone blasts your favorite song and dances with you all crazy crazy.

16

"Welcome to Love Love Bakery!" says Jane when someone new walks in.

The woman looks around. She spies the worn-in couches, smells the sharp scent of freshly ground coffee beans, and savors the sight of purple daisies, which remind her of home.

"I just moved here," she says.

"This place is exactly what you've been looking for," says Jane, and she introduces the woman to a bakery regular.

John gives Jane a fist bump. "Way to make her feel welcome," says John.

"It's the *yeast* I can do," says Jane with a chuckle.

John smiles, shakes his head, and walks back to the kitchen.

17

In the late morning, the bakery overflows with motion and commotion.

It's just a little nuts, thinks Jane. *But that's how we like it.*

18

Mamas talk about their vegetable gardens, the businesses they are building, and the books they are reading. Children nibble biscuits thick with jam and play with wooden toys. Snuggled on his mother's chest, a baby drinks milk. His snoozy eyes close.

Crowded around a long table, people study, read poetry, plan sermons and peaceful protests, and catch up over **avocado toast**.

Someone is writing a story, and someone is painting one.

"It's a full house today," says John, slurping his **chai**.

Jane's eyes twinkle. "You ain't seen *muffin* yet."

John finally laughs so hard that chai sprays from his nose.

Two pies fly from his arms.

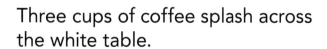

Three cups of coffee splash across the white table.

Four books are soggy and ruined.

Five dogs howl, waking
the snoozy baby.

Six jammy biscuits twirl through the air.

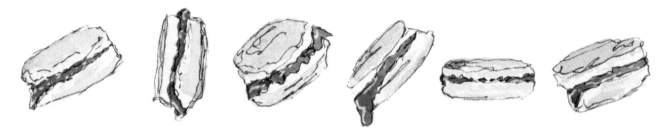

Seven jelly jars filled with flowers clatter to the floor.

Eight book club members shout over all the noise.

Nine drinks get switched.

Everyone in the long line huffs and puffs and shuffles.

The bakery is an epic mess. Jane looks around. "Yikes. Maybe this is too nuts."

"*Doughn*'t worry about it, Jane!" says John. "Get it? *Doughn*'t? Like bread dough!"

The book club members mop up the tea and coffee. The dogs beat the broom to the pie and biscuits. With the fallen flowers, John teaches customers how to braid daisy chains.

People try their mixed-up drinks.

"Whatever this is,
I love it!"

"Yuck! Coffee!"

"Mmm, my new favorite!"

A bakery is a place where mix-ups
and mayhem can sometimes
be magic.

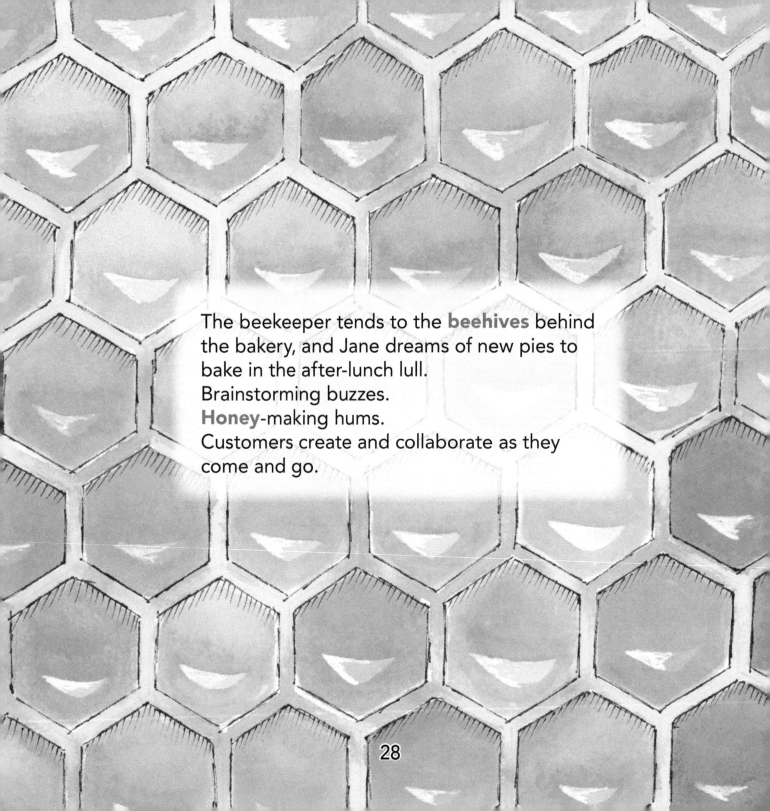

The beekeeper tends to the **beehives** behind the bakery, and Jane dreams of new pies to bake in the after-lunch lull.
Brainstorming buzzes.
Honey-making hums.
Customers create and collaborate as they come and go.

In the afternoon, Leo and his friends return from school. "Looks like it went nuts again," he sighs.

"What should we do?" asks Jane.

"Well, maybe not let everybody in? No babies. Definitely, no dogs. The bakery is like our home, and every day it gets wrecked."

Jane points to the sign on the door. *All* are welcome. "I hear you, bud. It is our home. But it's their home, too: the music makers and the mess makers. Without them, we'd have no flavor, no growth," says Jane. "Just like—"

"Just like sourdough," says Leo.

"When you fling your doors wide open, love gets in like wild yeast. And we all rise."

Tomorrow, the bakers will wake up early again. They will brew coffee and bake bread in an old blue house under a thick oak tree. Love Love Bakery will buzz with new ideas and hum with good work.

It will sing with,
"Good morning!"
"How are you?"
"Tell me your story."
And, "Have a beautiful day!"

31

Glossary

avocado – A fruit with buttery green flesh, which can be eaten sliced, mashed, or chopped, or it can be mixed with tomatoes, cilantro, and lime to make guacamole.

avocado toast – Toast with avocado on top. What did you think it was?

barista – A person who makes drinks with coffee, espresso, and tea.

bee hive – Human-made or bee-made houses where bees live, raise young bee babies, cook dinner, take out the trash, deposit honey, and make wax.

chai – A blend of tea and spices made with milk or water, sweetened with honey or sugar. An ancient drink with Indian and Thai origins. Originally chai did not contain tea leaves. "Chai" means tea. When you say "chai tea," you are saying "tea tea."

coffee – Coffee is brewed many different ways. Brewing means straining boiling water through ground coffee beans.

coffee bean – Coffee begins as a "cherry" growing on a coffee tree. It is dried and roasted before being ground and brewed into coffee.

cream – Cream made from cow's milk is the rich layer of milky butterfat skimmed from the top of milk. Some people do not drink cow's milk. They might add cashew cream to their coffee.

dough vs. batter – Batters and doughs are both mixtures of liquids and solids. They are both baked. Batters are wetter and can usually be poured. Doughs are drier and can be kneaded. Doughs have yeast. Batters do not. Hey, batter, batter, batter.

espresso – Strong coffee served in tiny cups called shots or mixed with milk or water.

first rise – After ingredients are mixed and kneaded, bread dough rests and grows. Later, it will be punched down and shaped into loaves.

honey – A sweet golden liquid produced by bees. Honey is a combination of flower nectar and a special bee enzyme.

hot chocolate – Chocolate melted into warm milk. Try adding peppermint.

kneading – After wet and dry dough ingredients are combined, the mixture becomes less sticky and more stretchy. Then, it is kneaded—rolled, folded, twirled, punched, or even spun in the air until it feels right.

kombucha – A fun-to-say fizzy fermented tea "come-BOO-cha!"

morning drink – A warm drink to start the day. How about steamed milk with honey and cinnamon? Or a cup of tea?

pretzel – A twisted knot of dough that takes a baking-soda bath before baking.

second rise – Inside the loaves of dough, yeast eat sugar and create air bubbles which fill the dough like thousands of little balloons.

sourdough bread – Bread that rises naturally using wild yeast in the environment. You can find wild yeast at stores, too, floating in the air and hanging around the stinky cheese, but you cannot buy it.

whisk – You whisk with a whisk and spoon with a spoon, so why don't you knife with a knife?

Let's Make Pretzels Today!

Here is a recipe that little bakers can make with their favorite grown-up.

Ingredients
- 2 cups warm water
- 1½ tablespoons yeast
- ¼ cup sugar (brown sugar, maple syrup, coconut sugar, or honey are great alternatives)
- 4 tablespoons melted butter or oil
- 3 teaspoons salt
- 4½ cups flour, more or less as needed

Cinnamon sugar topping:
- ⅓ cup baking soda
- 3 cups warm water
- 4 tablespoons butter or oil
- ½ cup sugar (coconut sugar is an alternative)
- 2 teaspoons cinnamon

In a large bowl, stir yeast into warm water. When it is bubbly, stir in brown sugar, melted butter or oil, salt, and one cup of flour. **Whisk**. Stir in three more cups of flour, one at a time until well-combined.

Place the dough onto a clean, floured work surface to knead. Add up to a half cup more flour as needed while you work.

Stop **kneading** once the dough feels stretchy, smooth, and slightly sticky. It should spring back when you press it. Return it to the bowl and cover with a towel.

Let the dough rise one hour or until it has grown twice its size. Use this time to read the book all over again or fling your own doors wide open and invite all the neighbor kids over to play.

When the rising hour is almost over, preheat the oven to 450 degrees. Combine 1/3 cup of baking soda with 3 cups of warm water. Whisk together to dissolve the baking soda. Place parchment paper on baking sheets.

When the dough has doubled, plop it onto a floured counter and gently knead into a log about 8 inches long. Using a pizza cutter, cut long strips from the dough about an inch wide. Roll the strip into a snake about 20 inches long without over-working or tearing the dough.

Make a U-shape with the snake. Twist the arms of the U twice around the middle and then fold the pretzel arms down. Or try shaping the dough into letters, shapes, or our favorite—pretzel ponies.

Dip pretzel in the baking soda bath. Set it on a towel to soak up moisture from the bottom of the pretzel. Place pretzel on baking sheet.

For salty pretzels, sprinkle with coarse salt before baking.

Bake pretzels for 7 minutes. Rotate baking sheet 180 degrees and then bake a few more minutes or until deep golden brown. Brush with melted butter.

For cinnamon sugar pretzels, combine sugar and cinnamon on a plate. Place baked, buttered pretzel face down in the cinnamon sugar mix. Shake off excess and dance around all crazy crazy with pretzel in hand.

Acknowledgments

This book would not exist without the encouragement of my family and friends.

Mitch Mitchell, I love the quiet enduring way you love and cheer me on. Thank you to Carolyn Madison for adding up my numbers and always taking my call. Thank you to my parents, Desiree Lacy and Michael Triana, and to my Granny, for always being in my corner. Thank you, Walt and Ruth Ann Mitchell, for watching my girls while I wrote the book. Thank you, Aunt Sarah, for putting books in my hands. Thank you, Anabelle, for making the pretzel recipe with me and listening to every draft. Thanks to everyone who read a draft. Thank you, Clementine, for sleeping! Thanks to my girlfriends, especially Jane Wild, for pouring your light and love into me. Thank you, Joe and Helen Thompson, for your edits and sourdough knowledge! A big thank you to Hayley for taking a chance on this first-time author. Your work is gorgeous and so are you. Thank you to Sarah for adding your gift of design. Thank you, Nick Courtright, for the merciless edits. And thank you to the whole team at Lucid Books!

Thanks also to John Blankemeyer, Maxx Wild, and everyone who allowed us to illustrate you. You made this bakery a wild home for all.

The heroes of Love Love Bakery are our 180 FABULOUS Kickstarter backers. You believed in this work and you made it happen. I will never forget your kindness.

Thank you especially to Brooke and Travis Beaty, Barry Haynes, DocFather and MareMare, Aaron and Corina Thompson, Tiffany Bledsoe, Londa Carlisle, Daryl and Holly Lacy, Peggy Renfroe, Clara Atkinson, Meg and Matthew Porter, Guest 132, Kris Black, Peter and Breanna Murray, Carrie-Leigh and Drew Cloutier, Kristin Adiska, Tiffany Campbell, Summer and Jacob Copple, Terah Moxley, Karen Reade, Savannah Brown, Meredith Alexander, Lynda and Howard Reed, Mike and Laurie Rufe, Michael and Karen Ruse, Drs. David and Deemie Naugle, Suellen Smith, Buck and Beth Holden, Frank McCawley and Daniela Grob, Sherri Johnson McDonald, Nicole Horton, Ali and Janice Cook, Glenn Orman, Callan Searcy and Patrick Reidy, Stacey DeMyer, Amanda King and Henri Ndaya, Mark and Melissa Bloom and Macy Bloom, Sarah and Dennis Stovall, Katie Pitts, Michelle Welch, Susan Losavio, Amera Collins, Luke and Adriann Ragsdale, Robert Ortiz, Garth and Kristi Hope, Richard and Mary Jane Madison, Carol Ruminski, Quentin and Michelle Manuel, the LaRovere family (whose pledge made us reach our funding goal!), Irene and David Harris, Charlie and Linda Harris, John and Christy Surgett, Johny Rosa, Blake and Jennifer Carlisle, and William Gerding (whose generosity made the final hours of the campaign a night to remember!).

Gratitude and love are all I have for you beautiful people.

The Bakery behind the Book

Love Love Bakery is a celebration of gathering spaces I have visited everywhere—friendly bakeries and coffee shops with doors wide open to all.

But above all, it celebrates a real place and real people. The first time I walked into Jane & John Dough Bakery at 208 N. Elm St. in Tomball, Texas, I was greeted by the real Jane's magical smile and a warm hello. It felt like home. That moment was the first spark of inspiration for this book.

Bakers Jane Wild and John Blankemeyer are serious about artisanal baking, strong coffee, and creating community among their regulars and visitors. All the illustrations are based on them and their beautiful shop—an old blue house under a giant tree in Old Town Tomball.

If you are ever in the area, stop by for a slice of salted honey pie. This place is exactly what you've been looking for.

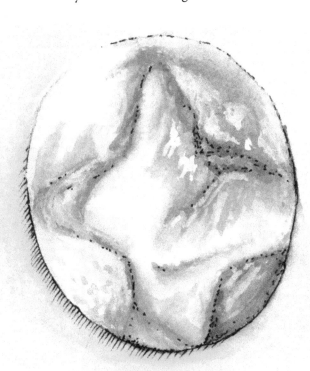

About the Author and Illustrator

Sara Triana Mitchell is a writer, editor, and poet. She loves picture books and coffee dates with her husband, Mitch. They live near Houston with their two daughters, two cats, and one Airedale Terrier. You can connect with Sara on Instagram (@saratrianamitchell) and at saratrianamitchell.com.

H2 Alaska, also known as **Hayley Haynes**, is an artist in Tomball, Texas. She has taught many art classes for children, including drawing, knitting, and woodworking. This is the first book she has illustrated; you can find her exploring new mediums on Facebook and Instagram (@h2_alaska).

Visit us and find books, morning drink mugs, letterpress prints, and postcards to send to a friend at **lovelovebakery.com**.

CPSIA information can be obtained
at www.ICGtesting.com
Printed in the USA
LVHW01*0829230518
578156LV00002B/4/P